Christopher March
Aptos, Calif.

Moto-Cross Racing

Written and photographed by
DAVID-LINN SEAVER

J. B. LIPPINCOTT COMPANY   Philadelphia and New York

Acknowledgment

The author wishes to acknowledge the aid and cooperation of William M. Bagnall, past president of the American Motorcycle Association.   D.-L.S.

U.S. Library of Congress Cataloging in Publication Data

Seaver, David-Linn, birth date
  Moto-cross racing.

   SUMMARY: Describes the rules and techniques of moto-cross racing and the construction of the motorcycles used in the events.

  1. Motorcycle racing—Juvenile literature. [1. Motorcycle racing] I. Title.
GV1060.S4   796.7'5   78-38590
ISBN-0-397-31294-6   ISBN-0-397-31226-1 (lib. bdg.)

Copyright © 1972 by David-Linn Seaver
All rights reserved
Printed in the United States of America
First edition

Moto-cross racing! The newest and most exciting style of motorcycle racing today has captured the attention of American motorcycle enthusiasts. It is truly a test of man and machine.

Although moto-cross racing has become popular in the United States only within the last few years, it is already an established national sport throughout Europe. Moto-cross racing began near Paris in the late 1940s and became officially organized in 1952. Today, European moto-cross events attract crowds of over twenty thousand fans.

Moto-cross racing was destined to find its way to the shores of America. We have over 4 million motorcycle riders, and these enthusiasts are always searching for new styles and methods of racing to further test themselves and their machines.

A moto-cross event consists of two or three heats, referred to as "motos," each of which lasts between fifteen and forty-five minutes. The rider who collects the most points for his finishes in each moto is declared the overall winner. With so much time to complete each race, a rider can spill, remount, catch the "pack"— and still place high in the standings.

Moto-cross racing is staged on a closed course of natural, rough terrain. Dangerous obstacles are cleared from the track. But gullies, hills, water holes, and gutted, sharp corners are very much a part of a moto-cross event. The track is usually not shorter than ½ mile or longer than 1½ miles. The width of the course ranges between 6 feet and 20 feet.

In keeping with the use of natural terrain, weather is also taken as it comes. Heavy rain or scorching hot desert sun doesn't halt the race. Riders force themselves to adapt to all riding conditions to gain those valuable points.

Moto-cross events are divided into classes according to the engine displacement of the motorcycles. The engines are measured in cubic centimeters (cc). There are classes for motorcycles with engine displacements from 125 cc to 500 cc. The most popular are the 250 cc and 500 cc classes.

Whether small or large, all moto-cross machines have two characteristics in common: they have special suspension systems which cushion the ride over the grueling course, and the motorcycles are extremely light. Even the largest motorcycle raced in moto-cross competition weighs about 250 pounds. Moto-crossers can cost from $300 for the small size up to $1,400 for the larger motorcycles.

Special moto-cross frames are available for separate purchase by anyone who wishes to assemble his own motorcycle. Some engines are available for this purpose, but a racer may use any power plant he wishes. The rider who buys a moto-crosser in kit form can spend as much or as little money on his machine as his budget allows.

The rider operates the clutch with his left hand and the front brake and throttle with his right hand, shifts gears with his left foot, and with his right foot controls the rear brake. Some moto-cross machines have five-speed transmissions. During the course of a moto the rider is constantly working these controls. Coordination is a key factor in motorcycle racing.

Events are divided into classes according to the size of the motorcycles, and each class into Juniors and Seniors. Juniors are those riders just beginning moto-cross racing; Seniors are the more experienced riders.

The new, exciting sport has attracted enthusiasts of all ages, from fifteen years up, into its ranks. Nearly every weekend well over seventy-five such events are staged around the nation all year round. These events are sponsored by local clubs, and often require membership in these clubs in order to race.

Preparation of a moto-cross machine is extremely important. The condition of the motorcycle often determines whether a rider finishes a race or is forced back into the pits for repairs. Crews spend many hours checking and rechecking the machines to insure that the rider can finish and collect his points. The machines are built strictly for moto-cross racing and need no modification.

Some of the machines have their own specific names. The Husqvarna is known as Husky, Hodaka builds the Super Rat, the Bultaco is called a Bull, and a "thoroughbred" racing machine built in Czechoslovakia is known in racing circles simply as the CZ.

Clothing is vitally important to the racers. The colorful clothes add to the excitement of racing, and protect riders from flying rocks which are picked up by knobby tires and hurled into the air. Many riders wear leather pants with ample padding, and sweat shirts to keep them cool during the vigorous physical workout of racing.

Moto-cross racing is so vigorous, in fact, that it is second only to soccer as the most physically demanding sport in the world. Riders in a moto-cross event use every ounce of strength and skill, often facing extremely rough terrain and weather conditions.

The speed of the motorcycles causes rocks to fly into the air, and some riders wear mouth guards, chest protectors, and shin guards. Other protective devices, such as shoulder pads and kidney belts, are also used by the riders.

Though the rider has approximately thirty minutes to complete one moto, the start is very important. The rider's tension shows as he eyes the starter who will drop the flag. To win he must complete more laps in a specific time than any other rider in his class.

Events featuring some classes of machines have as many as forty riders pounding over the terrain to reach the front of the pack before that first corner. Out in front, a rider does not have to "eat" dust, mud, or rocks.

Much of the track is so rough that riders find it easier to maneuver the machines if they stand on the foot pegs. The machines are built to steer easily in this position. Standing on the pegs also is less grueling for the rider and gives him a better view of the track.

Balance, ability, and stamina are tested in moto-cross racing. The rider must race hard over the roughest of terrain, stay on top of his machine, and stay ahead of the man breathing hard down his neck. The racer's motto might be, "Race as fast as you can for as long as you can."

Riders plow their way through soft corners, shooting rooster tails of dust and rocks behind them. Because visibility is poor, a rider has to know the track to stay on the course. Riders are given a few laps to practice and "feel out" the track before racing begins.

An experienced rider adds showmanship to this fast, colorful sport by throwing his bike sideways, cocking the front wheel as he comes skimming over a jump. The novice should not attempt to perform this maneuver. Balance and a feel for the machine and course are essential before "stunts" can be attempted.

The demanding terrain and high speeds do take their toll. Although there have been very few serious falls, riders are reminded that bad spills do occur.

Most moto-cross events are amateur events where the rewards for finishing in the top three places are trophies. In 1969, the American Motorcycle Association, the governing body of motorcycle racing in the United States, officially adopted new rules for moto-cross racing. Under A.M.A. sanction, purses which sometimes exceed $5,000 transform a local Sunday race into a highly competitive professional event.

Spectators and riders mingle in the pit area. Riders work on their machines while the fans wander from crew to crew to see the newest of moto-cross equipment.

After a moto the riders take what rest they can.

A major complaint lodged against motorcycles today is that they make too much noise. The motorcycle industry and the local motorcycle clubs realize that this problem must be solved. Many motorcycle clubs now rule that every machine in competition must have a silencer connected to the exhaust pipe to cut down offensive noise.

Motorcycle clubs believe that the old adage, "Noise equals power," will lose its appeal. Many racers are convinced that a well-tuned moto-crosser will go faster than a machine fitted with a noisy exhaust system.

Even though hot, tired, and physically drained at the end of a day, the rider will be back at the track next weekend for another go at moto-cross racing.